TISSUE BOX COVERS

CW00816025

LEISURE ARTS, INC. • Little Rock, Arkansas

LIGHTHOUSE

SET SAIL WITH this nautical-themed tissue box cover! Featuring four different lighthouse styles in bright summer colors, the cheerful design will give a by-the-bay feeling to any room.

SIDE 1

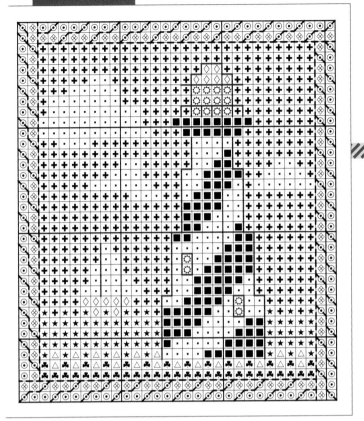

SIDE 2

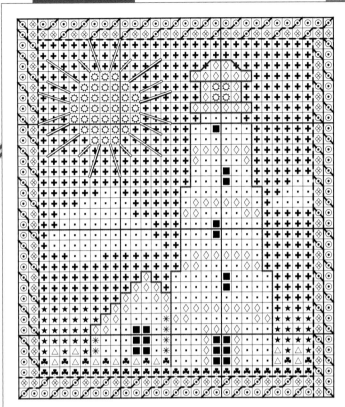

COLOR KEY

■	Black
✿	Bright Yellow
★	Dark Blue
♥	Dark Red
☉	Gold
♣	Green
✚	Light Blue
✳	Light Gray
△	Lime Green
◇	Red
·	White
⬧	Yellow

<u>Backstitch Floss (4 strands)</u>

──────── Black

── ── ── Light Brown

<u>Straight Stitch Floss (4 strands)</u>

━━━━━━ Yellow

Overcast the lighthouse edges with matching adjacent colors. Overcast all other edges and join together using Gold yarn.

SIDE 3

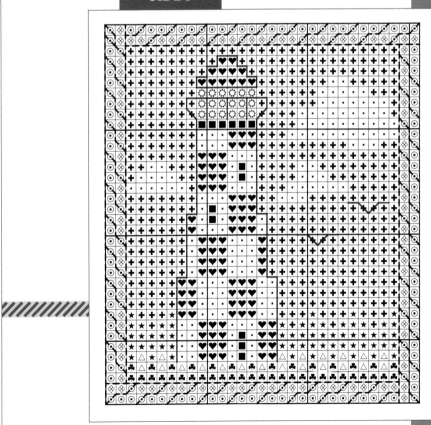

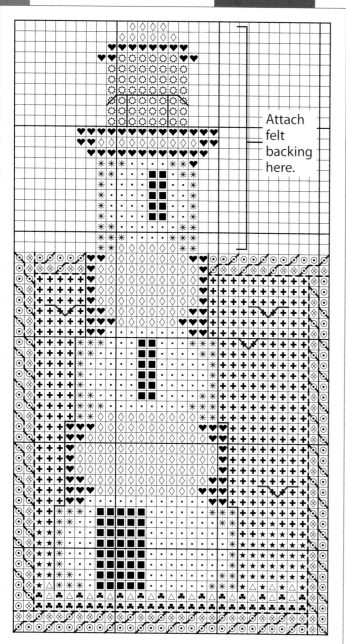

Attach felt backing here.

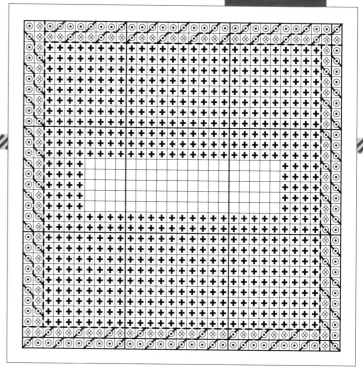

COLOR KEY

■	Black
✿	Bright Yellow
★	Dark Blue
♥	Dark Red
⊙	Gold
♣	Green
✚	Light Blue
✳	Light Gray
△	Lime Green
◇	Red
·	White
◈	Yellow

<u>Backstitch Floss (4 strands)</u>

———	Black
– – –	Light Brown

<u>Straight Stitch Floss (4 strands)</u>

══	Yellow

Overcast the lighthouse edges with matching adjacent colors. Overcast all other edges and join together using Gold yarn.

4

BIRDHOUSE GARDEN

BRIGHTEN UP A coffee table or dresser with this pretty tissue box cover. Three birdhouse designs, a sweet songbird, and lovely flowers make this the perfect addition to your springtime décor.

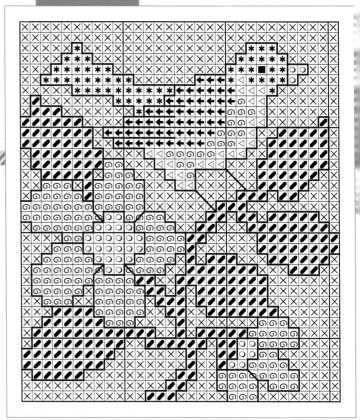

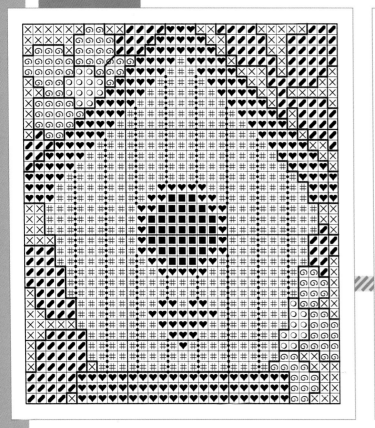

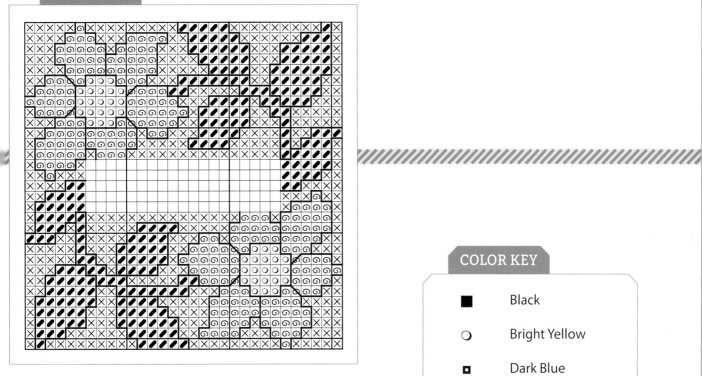

COLOR KEY

■	Black
○	Bright Yellow
▫	Dark Blue
+	Dark Red
◁	Ecru
×	Light Blue
←	Light Brown
#	Light Pink
✎	Lime Green
♥	Red
✱	Tan
᧒	White

Backstitch Floss (4 strands)

——	Black
∿∿∿	Dark Blue
·······	Red

Overcast the edges and join together using Light Blue yarn.

EVENING BLOSSOM

THIS ELEGANT TISSUE box cover will have you delighting in the beauty of garden blooms. Soft blue, lavender, and pink blossoms look stunning against a dramatic black background. Each side is different, making this piece a beauty from any angle.

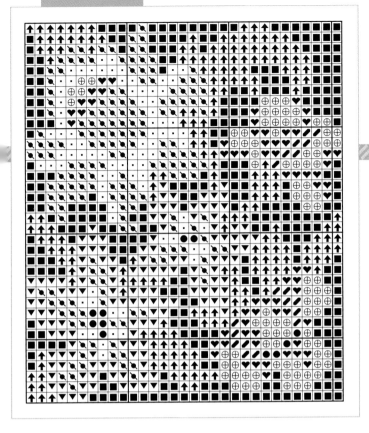

COLOR KEY

- ■ Black
- ● Bright Yellow
- ▪ Dark Blue
- ▰ Dark Red
- ▼ Lavender
- ◣ Light Blue
- ⊕ Light Pink
- ♥ Rose
- ↑ Sage
- ✿ Yellow

Overcast the edges and join together using Black yarn.

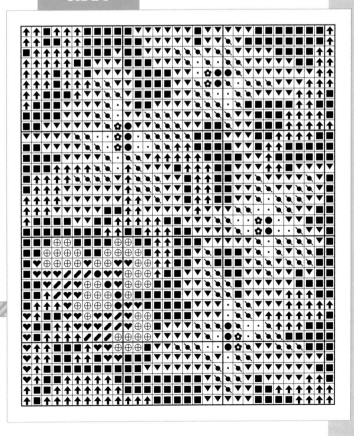

9

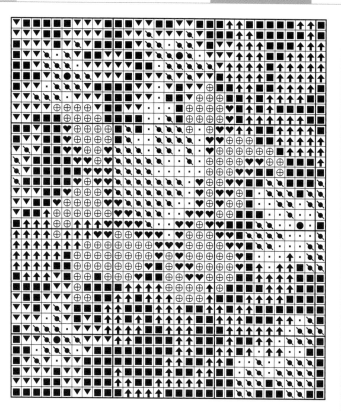

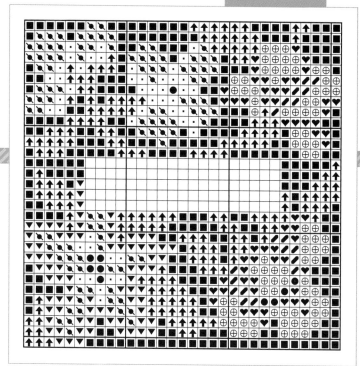

COLOR KEY

- ■ Black
- ● Bright Yellow
- · Dark Blue
- ▰ Dark Red
- ▼ Lavender
- ❧ Light Blue
- ⊕ Light Pink
- ♥ Rose
- ↑ Sage
- ✿ Yellow

Overcast the edges and join together using Black yarn.

KITTY

CREATE THIS ADORABLE kitty tissue box cover for your favorite cat lover! The sweet yellow tabby features a dimensional look with the face and tail, and would also look cute in a child's room.

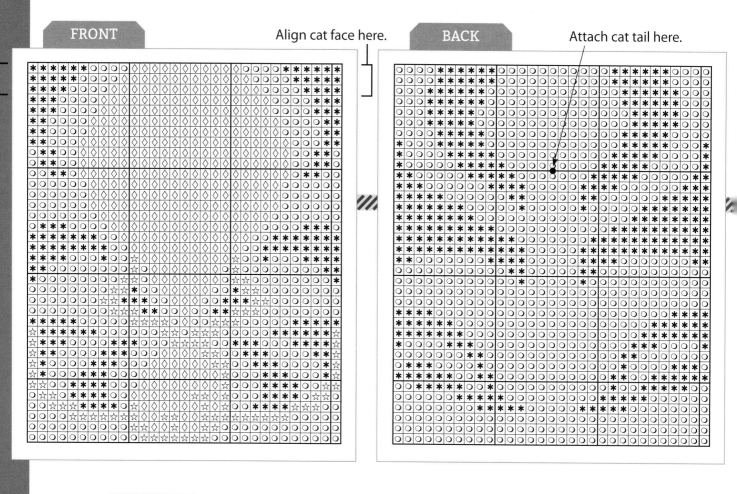

FRONT

Align cat face here.

BACK

Attach cat tail here.

COLOR KEY

▲ Black

◇ Cream

✳ Gold

✖ Light Pink

☆ Medium Brown

◑ Yellow

French Knot (Yarn)

● White

Straight Stitch Floss (4 strands)

——— Light Brown

Overcast the edges and join together with matching adjacent colors.

TOP

Cat Head and Tail Assembly

Cut felt slightly smaller than the cat head and tail. Secure to the back with felt glue or hot glue. After you join the tissue box side and top pieces together, attach the tail and face with felt glue or hot glue (refer to the stitching chart for placement).

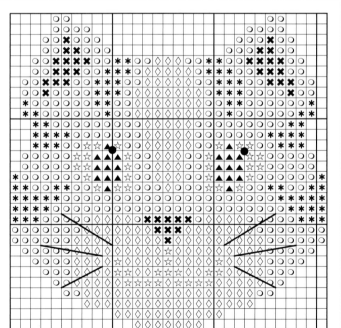

Attach
to front
of body
here.

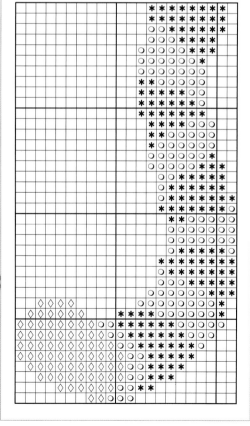

COUNTRY QUILT

THIS COLORFUL COUNTRY quilt design will brighten any room all year long. With a scalloped stripe across the bottom and bright quilted-look diamonds on the top, this tissue box cover will fit into many décor styles.

SIDE 1 (STITCH 2)

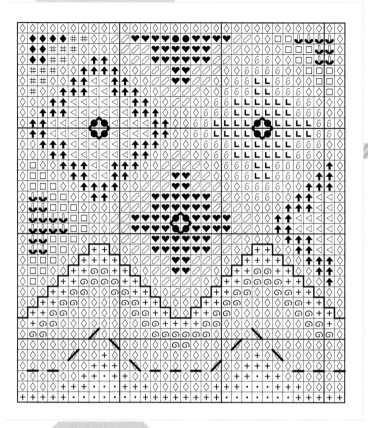

SIDE 2 (STITCH 2)

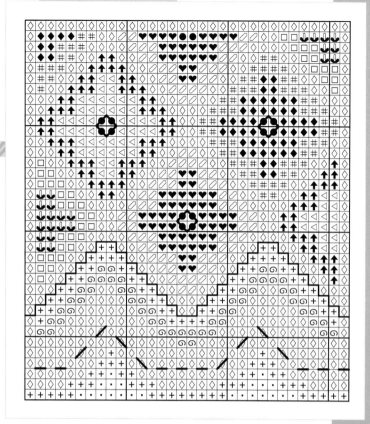

COLOR KEY

◇	Cream	⚓	Medium Yellow Green
L	Dark Blue	□	Pale Green
◆	Dark Purple	●	Pale Yellow
♥	Dark Red	⬭	Rose
◁	Gold	↻	Tan
#	Lavender	·	White
6	Light Blue	↑	Yellow
+	Light Brown		

Backstitch Floss (4 strands)

——————— Dark Brown: rickrack outline

——————— Light Blue: center of blue diamonds

——————— Rose: center of pink diamonds

——————— Violet: center of purple diamonds

——————— Yellow: center of yellow diamonds

Running Stitch Floss (4 strands)

- - - - Light Brown

Overcast the edges and join together using Cream yarn.

TOP

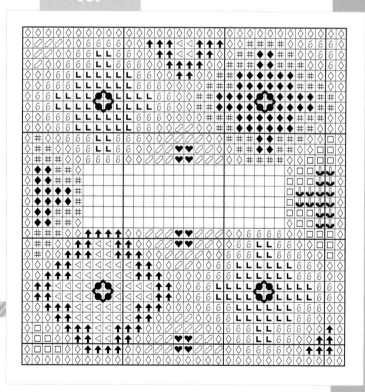

15

PIANO CONCERTO

THIS ELEGANT TISSUE box cover will look equally as lovely on top of a piano as it will atop a dresser. A single rose combined with graceful piano keys make this the perfect gift for classical music enthusiasts.

SIDE (STITCH 4)

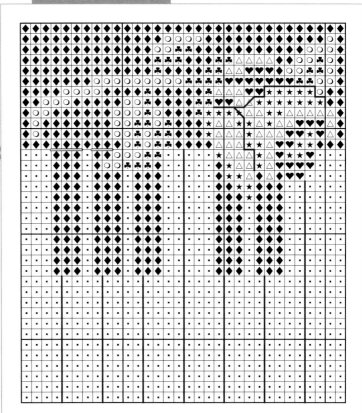

COLOR KEY

◆	Black
♥	Dark Red
◗	Pale Green
★	Red
△	Rose
·	White
♣	Yellow Green

Backstitch Floss (4 strands)

——— Black

═══ Dark Gray

Overcast the edges and join together with matching adjacent colors.

TOP

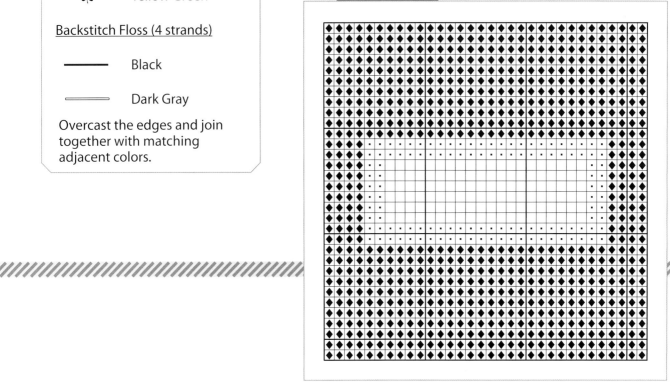

BUTTERFLY

BRIGHT SUMMERTIME BLOOMS and a three-dimensional butterfly accent give this tissue box cover a striking look. Make this as a gift for an avid gardener, or create it for yourself to add a natural touch to your décor.

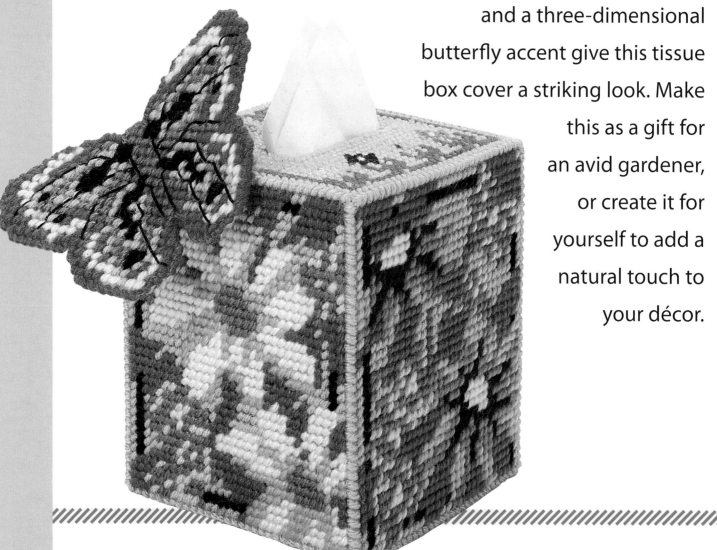

SIDE 1

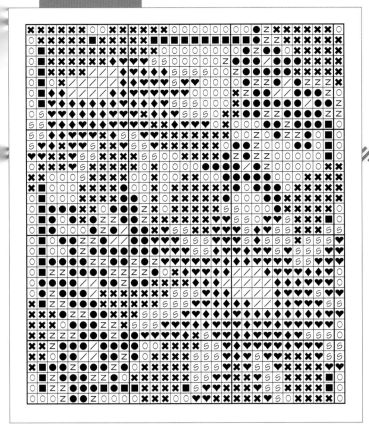

SIDE 2

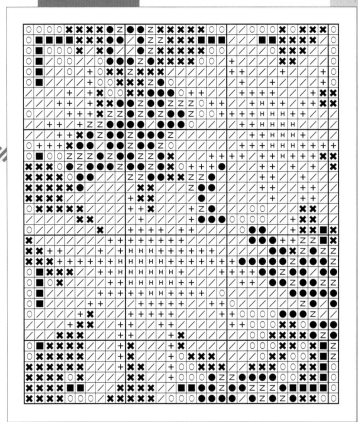

COLOR KEY

■	Black
/	Bright Yellow
●	Dark Blue
◆	Dark Red
+	Gold
✖	Green
↑	Lavender
Z	Light Blue
H	Light Brown
S	Light Pink
O	Lime Green
↑	Orange
♥	Rose

<u>Backstitch Floss (4 strands)</u>

—	Black

SIDE 3

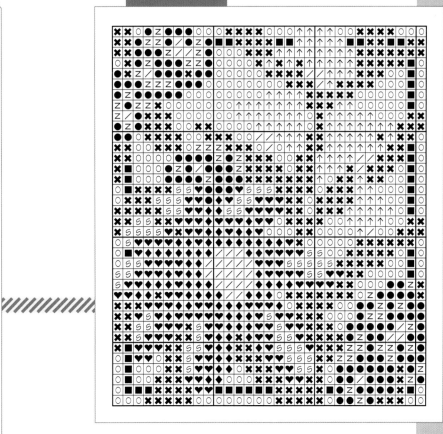

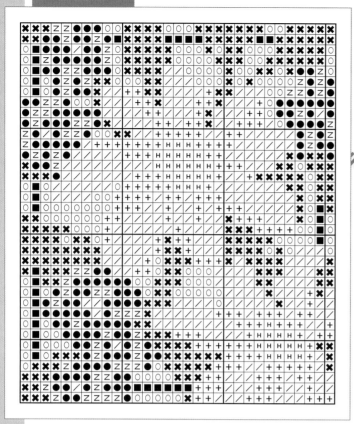

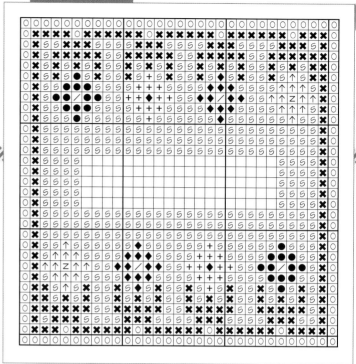

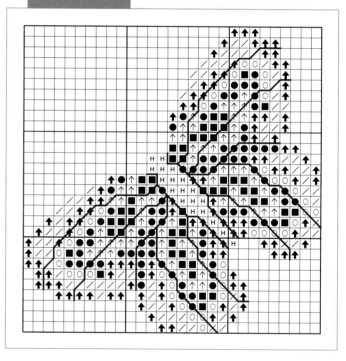

COLOR KEY

■	Black
╱	Bright Yellow
●	Dark Blue
◆	Dark Red
+	Gold
✖	Green
↑	Lavender
Z	Light Blue
H	Light Brown
S	Light Pink
○	Lime Green
↑	Orange
♥	Rose

Backstitch Floss (4 strands)

——— Black

Overcast the butterfly wings in Orange and the body in Light Brown.
Overcast the tissue box opening at the top with Pink.
Overcast the tissue box sides and join together with Lime Green.
Join the top of the box with Lime Green.

Butterfly Assembly
Cut felt slightly smaller than the trimmed butterfly. Secure to the back with felt glue or hot glue. Glue the butterfly to the top edge of the box, referring to the photo for placement.

SNOWBABIES

THIS MERRY AND bright tissue box cover is as fun to make as it is to give or display. Each side is different, giving you four adorable snowbabies in bright holiday colors. Celebrate the winter spirit and display it all season long.

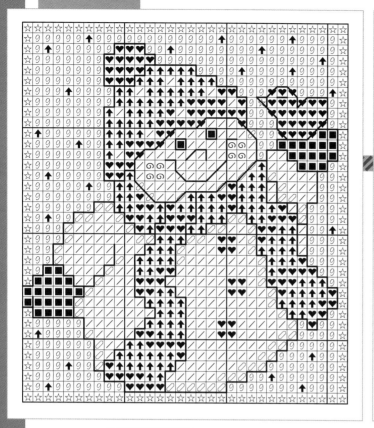

COLOR KEY

■	Black
☆	Bright Yellow
✚	Dark Blue
↑	Green
✿	Lavender
o	Light Blue
⬭	Light Gray
๑	Light Pink
9	Lime Green
♥	Red
/	White

<u>Backstitch Floss (4 strands)</u>

——	Black

Overcast the edges and join together using Bright Yellow yarn.

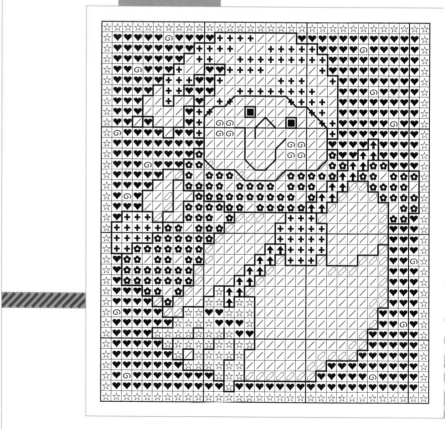

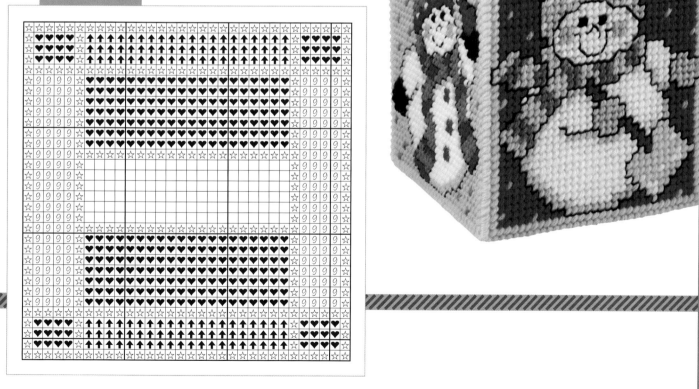

GENERAL INSTRUCTIONS

QUICK TIPS

1. Prior to beginning a project, look over the requirements and directions carefully.
2. Stitch the design on an uncut piece of plastic canvas to avoid snagging yarn or floss on ragged edges. If necessary, cover the edge with masking tape to avoid snags.
3. For a finished look, trim rough edges and cut off corners at an angle.

STARTING TO STITCH

All stitches begin on the back of your work. With a threaded needle, come up from the back of your work, hold a 1" section of the yarn against the back of the canvas and stitch over the 1" section. This will eliminate the need for a knot on the end of your yarn and will keep the back side of your work clean and flat. To finish off a color, run the needle under 4 or 5 stitches on the back and clip off. The tension of the stitches will hold the yarn in place and knots will not be necessary.

DIRECTIONS

- Stitch the piece(s). Except where otherwise indicated, ½ cross-stitch is used for all main areas.
- All pieces are stitched on 7- mesh plastic canvas using a size 16 tapestry needle and worsted weight yarn. Floss details use 4 strands of cotton embroidery floss.
- Cut away surplus canvas. Cut outside and trim the rough edges next to unworked edges. Overcast all edges.

CUTTING YOUR CANVAS

Always cut your canvas between the bars, making sure to leave one plastic bar between the stitches and cutting line. By cutting between the bars, you will be assured an adequate amount of plastic for overcasting the edges when finishing (see diagram).

ASSEMBLY

Using an overcast stitch, join the sides of the tissue box, then join the top; refer to each project for the yarn color to use for overcasting and joining. For projects that have a felt backing, cut felt slightly smaller than the trimmed plastic canvas project. Secure with felt glue or hot glue after project is assembled.

CLEANING

Hand-wash plastic canvas projects in warm water with a mild soap. Do not rub or scrub stitches, as this will cause the yarn to fuzz. Do not put your stitched piece in the dryer; allow to air dry.

STITCH GUIDE

½ Cross-Stitch

Most commonly used, it is either stitched in rows or columns. This stitch slants up from left to right. Always bring the needle up on odd numbers and down on even numbers.

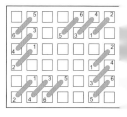

Overcast and Joining Stitch

This stitch is used for finishing your edges or joining two pieces of canvas. The stitch comes up in one hole, over the border bar and up the next hole, over the border bar and up the next hole. For joining, make sure the holes and edges are aligned before stitching.

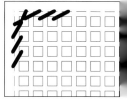

Backstitch

A backstitch is made in any direction with multiple continuous stitches crossing one bar at a time.

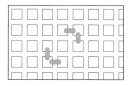

Straight Stitch

A straight stitch is formed by bringing the needle up at 1 and down at 2. The stitch can be of any length and worked in any direction.

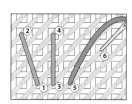

Running Stitch

To work this stitch, pass the needle over the yarn stitches on right side and under the back side of the canvas. Continue working these stitches of equal length in an even line, skipping every other space.

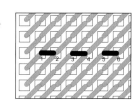

French Knot

Bring the threaded needle through the canvas and wrap the floss around the needle as shown. Tighten the twists and return the needle through the canvas at the same place. The floss will slide through the wrapped thread to make the knot.

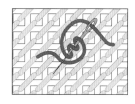

Produced by Herrschners, Inc., for distribution exclusively by Leisure Arts, Inc., 5701 Ranch Drive, Little Rock, Arkansas 72223-9633, leisurearts.com.

We have made every effort to ensure that these instructions are accurate and complete. We cannot, however, be responsible for human error, typographical mistakes, or variations in individual work.